50 BBQ Secrets for the Backyard Chef
Recipes for Home

By: Kelly Johnson

Table of Contents

- Classic BBQ Ribs
- Smoked Brisket
- Grilled Chicken Wings
- BBQ Pulled Pork
- Marinated Grilled Shrimp
- Beef Kabobs
- BBQ Pork Chops
- Honey-Glazed Salmon
- Grilled Vegetable Skewers
- BBQ Chicken Thighs
- Smoked Sausage
- BBQ Meatballs
- Sweet and Spicy BBQ Tofu
- Grilled Corn on the Cob
- Teriyaki Grilled Pineapple
- Cajun Grilled Catfish
- Maple-Glazed Brussels Sprouts
- BBQ Lamb Chops
- Chimichurri Grilled Flank Steak
- Spicy BBQ Cauliflower
- Herb-Marinated Grilled Portobello Mushrooms
- Jamaican Jerk Chicken
- BBQ Beef Brisket Sandwiches
- Smoked Turkey Legs
- Grilled Stuffed Peppers
- BBQ Veggie Burger
- Sweet BBQ Baked Beans
- Grilled Flatbread Pizza
- Spicy Garlic BBQ Shrimp Tacos
- Lemon-Herb Grilled Asparagus
- BBQ Chicken Pizza
- Grilled Zucchini and Squash
- Cherry Chipotle BBQ Sauce
- Applewood Smoked Pork Tenderloin
- Grilled Eggplant Roll-Ups

- Buffalo Cauliflower Bites
- BBQ Duck Breasts
- Grilled Peach Salad
- Cilantro Lime Grilled Chicken
- Smoky BBQ Chili
- Grilled Romaine Salad
- BBQ Shrimp and Grits
- Sriracha Honey Grilled Chicken
- Mediterranean Grilled Vegetable Platter
- BBQ Pulled Jackfruit Sandwiches
- Lemon Pepper Grilled Fish
- Chipotle BBQ Corn Salad
- Grilled Sweet Potatoes
- BBQ Chicken Nachos
- Smoked Mac and Cheese

Classic BBQ Ribs

Ingredients:

- **For the Ribs:**
    - 2 racks of pork ribs (baby back or spare ribs)
    - 1 tablespoon salt
    - 1 tablespoon black pepper
    - 1 tablespoon garlic powder
    - 1 tablespoon onion powder
    - 1 tablespoon smoked paprika (optional)
    - 1 teaspoon cayenne pepper (optional)
- **For the BBQ Sauce:**
    - 1 cup ketchup
    - 1/2 cup apple cider vinegar
    - 1/2 cup brown sugar
    - 1/4 cup honey
    - 2 tablespoons Worcestershire sauce
    - 1 tablespoon mustard
    - 1 tablespoon smoked paprika
    - 1 teaspoon garlic powder
    - 1 teaspoon onion powder
    - Salt and pepper to taste

Instructions:

1. **Prep the Ribs:**
    - Preheat your oven to 300°F (150°C).
    - Remove the silver skin from the back of the ribs.
    - Rub the ribs with salt, pepper, garlic powder, onion powder, smoked paprika, and cayenne. Let sit for 30 minutes.
2. **Cook the Ribs:**
    - Place the ribs on a lined baking sheet. Cover with foil.
    - Bake for 2.5 to 3 hours until tender.
3. **Make the BBQ Sauce:**
    - In a saucepan, combine all BBQ sauce ingredients over medium heat.
    - Bring to a simmer and let cook for 15-20 minutes. Adjust seasoning.
4. **Grill or Broil:**
    - Preheat your grill (or broiler) to medium-high.

- Brush BBQ sauce on the ribs and grill/broil for 5-10 minutes, turning and basting until caramelized.
5. **Serve:**
    - Let rest for a few minutes, then cut between the bones and serve with extra BBQ sauce.

Enjoy your BBQ ribs!

Smoked Brisket

Ingredients:

- 1 whole beef brisket (5-10 pounds)
- 2 tablespoons salt
- 2 tablespoons black pepper
- 1 tablespoon garlic powder
- 1 tablespoon onion powder
- 1 tablespoon smoked paprika
- Wood chips for smoking (oak or hickory)

Instructions:

1. **Prep the Brisket:** Trim excess fat from the brisket, leaving about 1/4 inch. Mix salt, pepper, garlic powder, onion powder, and smoked paprika. Rub the mixture all over the brisket. Let it rest for at least 1 hour (or overnight in the fridge).
2. **Smoke the Brisket:** Preheat your smoker to 225°F (107°C) and add wood chips. Place the brisket in the smoker, fat side up, and smoke for about 1 hour per pound or until the internal temperature reaches 195°F (90°C).
3. **Rest and Serve:** Wrap the brisket in foil and let it rest for at least 30 minutes before slicing. Serve with your favorite BBQ sauce.

Grilled Chicken Wings

Ingredients:

- 2 pounds chicken wings
- 2 tablespoons olive oil
- 1 tablespoon garlic powder
- 1 tablespoon onion powder
- 1 tablespoon smoked paprika
- Salt and pepper to taste
- Your favorite BBQ sauce for basting

Instructions:

1. **Prep the Wings:** In a large bowl, toss the wings with olive oil, garlic powder, onion powder, smoked paprika, salt, and pepper.
2. **Grill the Wings:** Preheat your grill to medium-high heat. Place the wings on the grill and cook for about 20-25 minutes, turning occasionally until crispy and cooked through.
3. **Baste and Serve:** In the last few minutes, brush the wings with BBQ sauce. Serve hot with extra sauce on the side.

BBQ Pulled Pork

Ingredients:

- 4-5 pounds pork shoulder (butt)
- 2 tablespoons salt
- 2 tablespoons black pepper
- 1 tablespoon garlic powder
- 1 tablespoon onion powder
- 1 tablespoon smoked paprika
- 1 cup BBQ sauce (for serving)

Instructions:

1. **Prep the Pork:** Rub the pork shoulder with salt, pepper, garlic powder, onion powder, and smoked paprika. Let it rest for at least 1 hour (or overnight).
2. **Cook the Pork:** Preheat your smoker or slow cooker to 225°F (107°C) and add wood chips if smoking. Cook for about 1.5 hours per pound, until the internal temperature reaches 195°F (90°C).
3. **Shred and Serve:** Remove the pork from the heat and let it rest for 30 minutes. Shred the meat using forks and mix with BBQ sauce. Serve on buns or with sides.

Enjoy your BBQ feast!

Marinated Grilled Shrimp

Ingredients:

- 1 pound large shrimp, peeled and deveined
- 1/4 cup olive oil
- 2 tablespoons lemon juice
- 3 cloves garlic, minced
- 1 teaspoon paprika
- Salt and pepper to taste
- Skewers (if using wooden skewers, soak in water for 30 minutes)

Instructions:

1. **Marinate the Shrimp:** In a bowl, mix olive oil, lemon juice, garlic, paprika, salt, and pepper. Add shrimp and toss to coat. Marinate for 30 minutes.
2. **Grill the Shrimp:** Preheat grill to medium-high heat. Thread shrimp onto skewers. Grill for 2-3 minutes on each side until pink and cooked through.

Beef Kabobs

Ingredients:

- 1.5 pounds beef sirloin, cut into 1-inch cubes
- 1/4 cup soy sauce
- 1/4 cup olive oil
- 2 tablespoons balsamic vinegar
- 2 tablespoons Worcestershire sauce
- 2 cloves garlic, minced
- Salt and pepper to taste
- Bell peppers, onions, and mushrooms, cut into chunks
- Skewers

Instructions:

1. **Marinate the Beef:** In a bowl, whisk together soy sauce, olive oil, balsamic vinegar, Worcestershire sauce, garlic, salt, and pepper. Add beef and marinate for at least 1 hour.
2. **Assemble Kabobs:** Thread beef and vegetables onto skewers.
3. **Grill the Kabobs:** Preheat grill to medium-high heat. Grill kabobs for 10-12 minutes, turning occasionally, until desired doneness.

BBQ Pork Chops

Ingredients:

- 4 bone-in pork chops
- 1 tablespoon olive oil
- Salt and pepper to taste
- 1 cup BBQ sauce

Instructions:

1. **Season the Chops:** Rub pork chops with olive oil, salt, and pepper.
2. **Grill the Chops:** Preheat grill to medium-high heat. Grill chops for 6-7 minutes per side, basting with BBQ sauce during the last few minutes, until cooked through.

Honey-Glazed Salmon

Ingredients:

- 4 salmon fillets
- 1/4 cup honey
- 2 tablespoons soy sauce
- 1 tablespoon Dijon mustard
- Salt and pepper to taste

Instructions:

1. **Prepare the Glaze:** In a bowl, whisk together honey, soy sauce, Dijon mustard, salt, and pepper.
2. **Marinate the Salmon:** Brush glaze over salmon fillets and let marinate for 15-30 minutes.
3. **Grill the Salmon:** Preheat grill to medium heat. Grill salmon for about 4-5 minutes per side, until cooked through and flaky.

Grilled Vegetable Skewers

Ingredients:

- 2 bell peppers, cut into chunks
- 1 zucchini, sliced
- 1 red onion, cut into wedges
- 8 cherry tomatoes
- 1/4 cup olive oil
- Salt and pepper to taste
- Skewers

Instructions:

1. **Prepare the Vegetables:** Toss vegetables with olive oil, salt, and pepper.
2. **Assemble Skewers:** Thread vegetables onto skewers.
3. **Grill the Skewers:** Preheat grill to medium heat. Grill skewers for about 10-12 minutes, turning occasionally until tender.

BBQ Chicken Thighs

Ingredients:

- 4 chicken thighs, bone-in and skin-on
- 1 tablespoon olive oil
- Salt and pepper to taste
- 1 cup BBQ sauce

Instructions:

1. **Season the Chicken:** Rub chicken thighs with olive oil, salt, and pepper.
2. **Grill the Thighs:** Preheat grill to medium heat. Grill chicken thighs skin side down for 6-7 minutes, then flip and cook for another 10-12 minutes, basting with BBQ sauce.

Smoked Sausage

Ingredients:

- 1 pound smoked sausage (such as kielbasa or andouille)
- Mustard or BBQ sauce for serving

Instructions:

1. **Prep the Sausage:** Slice sausage into 1-inch pieces or leave whole.
2. **Grill the Sausage:** Preheat grill to medium heat. Grill sausage for 6-8 minutes, turning occasionally until heated through. Serve with mustard or BBQ sauce.

BBQ Meatballs

Ingredients:

- 1 pound ground beef or turkey
- 1/2 cup breadcrumbs
- 1/4 cup grated Parmesan cheese
- 1 egg
- 2 cloves garlic, minced
- 1 teaspoon Italian seasoning
- Salt and pepper to taste
- 1 cup BBQ sauce

Instructions:

1. **Make the Meatballs:** In a bowl, mix ground meat, breadcrumbs, Parmesan, egg, garlic, Italian seasoning, salt, and pepper. Form into 1-inch meatballs.
2. **Grill the Meatballs:** Preheat grill to medium heat. Grill meatballs for 10-12 minutes, turning occasionally until cooked through. Brush with BBQ sauce during the last few minutes.

Enjoy your delicious BBQ spread!

Sweet and Spicy BBQ Tofu

Ingredients:

- 1 block (14 oz) firm tofu, drained and pressed
- 1/4 cup BBQ sauce
- 2 tablespoons honey or maple syrup
- 1 tablespoon sriracha (adjust for spice)
- 1 tablespoon soy sauce

Instructions:

1. **Prep the Tofu:** Cut tofu into thick slices or cubes.
2. **Make the Marinade:** In a bowl, mix BBQ sauce, honey, sriracha, and soy sauce.
3. **Marinate the Tofu:** Toss tofu in the marinade and let it sit for at least 30 minutes.
4. **Grill the Tofu:** Preheat grill to medium heat. Grill tofu for about 5-7 minutes per side until charred and heated through.

Grilled Corn on the Cob

Ingredients:

- 4 ears of corn, husked
- 4 tablespoons butter
- Salt to taste
- Optional: chili powder or parmesan cheese for topping

Instructions:

1. **Prep the Corn:** Husk the corn and remove silk.
2. **Grill the Corn:** Preheat grill to medium-high heat. Grill corn for 10-15 minutes, turning occasionally until tender and charred.
3. **Serve:** Brush with butter and sprinkle with salt (and optional toppings).

Teriyaki Grilled Pineapple

Ingredients:

- 1 fresh pineapple, peeled and sliced into rings
- 1/2 cup teriyaki sauce
- Optional: sesame seeds for garnish

Instructions:

1. **Marinate the Pineapple:** In a bowl, combine pineapple slices and teriyaki sauce. Let marinate for at least 15 minutes.
2. **Grill the Pineapple:** Preheat grill to medium heat. Grill pineapple for 3-4 minutes per side until caramelized.
3. **Serve:** Garnish with sesame seeds if desired.

Cajun Grilled Catfish

Ingredients:

- 4 catfish fillets
- 2 tablespoons Cajun seasoning
- 2 tablespoons olive oil
- Lemon wedges for serving

Instructions:

1. **Season the Fish:** Rub catfish fillets with Cajun seasoning and olive oil.
2. **Grill the Fish:** Preheat grill to medium-high heat. Grill catfish for about 4-5 minutes per side until cooked through and flaky.
3. **Serve:** Serve with lemon wedges.

Maple-Glazed Brussels Sprouts

Ingredients:

- 1 pound Brussels sprouts, halved
- 2 tablespoons olive oil
- 2 tablespoons maple syrup
- Salt and pepper to taste

Instructions:

1. **Prep the Brussels Sprouts:** Toss Brussels sprouts with olive oil, maple syrup, salt, and pepper.
2. **Grill the Sprouts:** Preheat grill to medium heat. Place sprouts in a grill basket or foil pouch. Grill for 15-20 minutes, turning occasionally until tender and caramelized.

BBQ Lamb Chops

Ingredients:

- 8 lamb chops
- 1/4 cup olive oil
- 2 tablespoons fresh rosemary, chopped
- 2 tablespoons garlic, minced
- Salt and pepper to taste
- 1/2 cup BBQ sauce for basting

Instructions:

1. **Marinate the Chops:** In a bowl, mix olive oil, rosemary, garlic, salt, and pepper. Rub the mixture over lamb chops and let marinate for at least 1 hour.
2. **Grill the Chops:** Preheat grill to medium-high heat. Grill lamb chops for about 4-5 minutes per side, basting with BBQ sauce.

Chimichurri Grilled Flank Steak

Ingredients:

- 1.5 pounds flank steak
- Salt and pepper to taste
- **For the Chimichurri:**
    - 1 cup fresh parsley, chopped
    - 1/4 cup red wine vinegar
    - 1/4 cup olive oil
    - 4 cloves garlic, minced
    - 1 teaspoon red pepper flakes
    - Salt and pepper to taste

Instructions:

1. **Make the Chimichurri:** In a bowl, combine parsley, red wine vinegar, olive oil, garlic, red pepper flakes, salt, and pepper. Mix well and set aside.
2. **Season the Steak:** Rub flank steak with salt and pepper.
3. **Grill the Steak:** Preheat grill to high heat. Grill steak for 5-7 minutes per side for medium-rare. Let rest for 5 minutes before slicing.
4. **Serve:** Drizzle chimichurri over sliced steak.

Spicy BBQ Cauliflower

Ingredients:

- 1 head cauliflower, cut into florets
- 1/4 cup BBQ sauce
- 1 tablespoon hot sauce (adjust for spice)
- 1 tablespoon olive oil
- Salt to taste

Instructions:

1. **Prep the Cauliflower:** In a bowl, toss cauliflower florets with olive oil, salt, BBQ sauce, and hot sauce.
2. **Grill the Cauliflower:** Preheat grill to medium heat. Place cauliflower in a grill basket and grill for 15-20 minutes, turning occasionally until tender and charred.

Enjoy your delicious grilled dishes!

Herb-Marinated Grilled Portobello Mushrooms

Ingredients:

- 4 large portobello mushrooms, stems removed
- 1/4 cup olive oil
- 2 tablespoons balsamic vinegar
- 2 cloves garlic, minced
- 1 tablespoon fresh rosemary, chopped
- 1 tablespoon fresh thyme, chopped
- Salt and pepper to taste

Instructions:

1. **Make the Marinade:** In a bowl, whisk together olive oil, balsamic vinegar, garlic, rosemary, thyme, salt, and pepper.
2. **Marinate the Mushrooms:** Place mushrooms in the marinade, coating well. Let sit for at least 30 minutes.
3. **Grill the Mushrooms:** Preheat grill to medium heat. Grill mushrooms for about 5-7 minutes per side until tender.

Jamaican Jerk Chicken

Ingredients:

- 4 chicken thighs (or breasts)
- 2 tablespoons jerk seasoning
- 2 tablespoons olive oil
- 1 lime, juiced

Instructions:

1. **Prep the Chicken:** Rub chicken with jerk seasoning, olive oil, and lime juice. Marinate for at least 1 hour.
2. **Grill the Chicken:** Preheat grill to medium-high heat. Grill chicken for 6-7 minutes per side until cooked through.

BBQ Beef Brisket Sandwiches

Ingredients:

- 2 pounds beef brisket
- 1 tablespoon salt
- 1 tablespoon black pepper
- 1 cup BBQ sauce
- Hamburger buns

Instructions:

1. **Season the Brisket:** Rub brisket with salt and pepper.
2. **Cook the Brisket:** Preheat smoker or grill to 225°F (107°C). Cook brisket for about 1.5 hours per pound until tender.
3. **Serve:** Shred brisket and mix with BBQ sauce. Serve on buns.

Smoked Turkey Legs

Ingredients:

- 4 turkey legs
- 2 tablespoons olive oil
- 2 tablespoons smoked paprika
- 1 tablespoon garlic powder
- Salt and pepper to taste

Instructions:

1. **Prep the Turkey Legs:** Rub turkey legs with olive oil, smoked paprika, garlic powder, salt, and pepper.
2. **Smoke the Turkey Legs:** Preheat smoker to 225°F (107°C). Smoke for 2.5-3 hours until internal temperature reaches 165°F (74°C).

Grilled Stuffed Peppers

Ingredients:

- 4 bell peppers, halved and seeds removed
- 1 cup cooked rice or quinoa
- 1 cup black beans, rinsed and drained
- 1 cup corn
- 1 cup salsa
- 1 cup shredded cheese (optional)

Instructions:

1. **Prepare the Filling:** In a bowl, mix rice, black beans, corn, and salsa.
2. **Stuff the Peppers:** Fill each pepper half with the mixture and top with cheese if desired.
3. **Grill the Peppers:** Preheat grill to medium heat. Wrap peppers in foil and grill for 20-25 minutes until tender.

BBQ Veggie Burger

Ingredients:

- 1 can (15 oz) black beans, drained and rinsed
- 1/2 cup breadcrumbs
- 1/4 cup onion, finely chopped
- 1/4 cup corn
- 1 teaspoon cumin
- Salt and pepper to taste
- Hamburger buns

Instructions:

1. **Make the Patties:** In a bowl, mash black beans. Mix in breadcrumbs, onion, corn, cumin, salt, and pepper. Form into patties.
2. **Grill the Patties:** Preheat grill to medium heat. Grill patties for 5-6 minutes on each side until heated through. Serve on buns.

Sweet BBQ Baked Beans

Ingredients:

- 2 cans (15 oz each) baked beans
- 1/2 cup BBQ sauce
- 1/4 cup brown sugar
- 1/4 cup diced onion
- 2 tablespoons mustard

Instructions:

1. **Combine Ingredients:** In a pot, mix baked beans, BBQ sauce, brown sugar, onion, and mustard.
2. **Heat:** Cook over medium heat until heated through, about 10-15 minutes. Serve warm.

Grilled Flatbread Pizza

Ingredients:

- 1 store-bought flatbread or pizza dough
- 1/2 cup marinara sauce
- 1 cup shredded mozzarella cheese
- Toppings of choice (pepperoni, vegetables, etc.)

Instructions:

1. **Prep the Flatbread:** Preheat grill to medium heat. Lightly oil one side of the flatbread.
2. **Grill the Flatbread:** Place oiled side down on the grill. Grill for 2-3 minutes until grill marks appear.
3. **Add Toppings:** Flip the flatbread, spread sauce, and add cheese and toppings. Close the lid and grill for an additional 3-5 minutes until cheese is melted.

Enjoy your delicious grilled creations!

Spicy Garlic BBQ Shrimp Tacos

Ingredients:

- 1 pound large shrimp, peeled and deveined
- 1/4 cup BBQ sauce
- 2 tablespoons olive oil
- 2 cloves garlic, minced
- 1 teaspoon cayenne pepper (adjust for spice)
- Corn or flour tortillas
- Toppings: avocado, cilantro, lime wedges, slaw

Instructions:

1. **Marinate the Shrimp:** In a bowl, mix BBQ sauce, olive oil, garlic, and cayenne pepper. Add shrimp and marinate for 30 minutes.
2. **Grill the Shrimp:** Preheat grill to medium-high heat. Grill shrimp for 2-3 minutes on each side until cooked through.
3. **Assemble Tacos:** Warm tortillas on the grill. Fill with shrimp and top with avocado, cilantro, lime juice, and slaw.

Lemon-Herb Grilled Asparagus

Ingredients:

- 1 bunch asparagus, trimmed
- 2 tablespoons olive oil
- 1 lemon, zested and juiced
- 2 cloves garlic, minced
- Salt and pepper to taste

Instructions:

1. **Prep the Asparagus:** In a bowl, whisk together olive oil, lemon zest, lemon juice, garlic, salt, and pepper. Add asparagus and toss to coat.
2. **Grill the Asparagus:** Preheat grill to medium heat. Grill asparagus for about 5-7 minutes, turning occasionally, until tender and slightly charred.

BBQ Chicken Pizza

Ingredients:

- 1 pizza crust (store-bought or homemade)
- 1 cup cooked chicken, shredded
- 1/2 cup BBQ sauce
- 1 cup shredded mozzarella cheese
- 1/4 cup red onion, thinly sliced
- Fresh cilantro for garnish

Instructions:

1. **Prepare the Chicken:** In a bowl, mix shredded chicken with BBQ sauce.
2. **Assemble the Pizza:** Preheat grill to medium heat. Spread BBQ chicken on the pizza crust, top with mozzarella and red onion.
3. **Grill the Pizza:** Place pizza on the grill and cover. Grill for about 10-15 minutes until cheese is melted and crust is golden. Garnish with cilantro.

Grilled Zucchini and Squash

Ingredients:

- 2 zucchini, sliced
- 2 yellow squash, sliced
- 2 tablespoons olive oil
- Salt and pepper to taste

Instructions:

1. **Prep the Vegetables:** Toss zucchini and squash with olive oil, salt, and pepper.
2. **Grill the Vegetables:** Preheat grill to medium heat. Grill for about 5-7 minutes per side until tender and charred.

Cherry Chipotle BBQ Sauce

Ingredients:

- 1 cup cherry preserves
- 1/2 cup ketchup
- 2 tablespoons apple cider vinegar
- 1 tablespoon chipotle in adobo sauce, minced
- 1 teaspoon garlic powder
- Salt and pepper to taste

Instructions:

1. **Combine Ingredients:** In a saucepan, mix cherry preserves, ketchup, apple cider vinegar, chipotle, garlic powder, salt, and pepper.
2. **Simmer:** Heat over medium heat, stirring occasionally, until warmed through. Use as a sauce for grilled meats.

Applewood Smoked Pork Tenderloin

Ingredients:

- 1.5 pounds pork tenderloin
- 2 tablespoons olive oil
- 1 tablespoon applewood smoked seasoning (or your favorite spice blend)
- Salt and pepper to taste

Instructions:

1. **Prep the Pork:** Rub pork tenderloin with olive oil, smoked seasoning, salt, and pepper.
2. **Smoke the Pork:** Preheat smoker or grill to 225°F (107°C) with applewood chips. Smoke pork for 2-3 hours until internal temperature reaches 145°F (63°C).
3. **Rest and Slice:** Let rest for 10 minutes before slicing.

Grilled Eggplant Roll-Ups

Ingredients:

- 1 large eggplant, sliced lengthwise
- 1 cup ricotta cheese
- 1/2 cup mozzarella cheese, shredded
- 1/4 cup fresh basil, chopped
- Salt and pepper to taste
- Marinara sauce for serving

Instructions:

1. **Prep the Eggplant:** Sprinkle eggplant slices with salt and let sit for 20 minutes. Rinse and pat dry. Brush with olive oil.
2. **Grill the Eggplant:** Preheat grill to medium heat. Grill eggplant for 3-4 minutes per side until tender.
3. **Assemble Roll-Ups:** Spread ricotta on each slice, sprinkle with mozzarella and basil, then roll up. Serve with marinara sauce.

Buffalo Cauliflower Bites

Ingredients:

- 1 head cauliflower, cut into florets
- 1 cup flour
- 1 cup water
- 1 teaspoon garlic powder
- 1 teaspoon paprika
- 1 cup buffalo sauce
- Optional: blue cheese dressing for dipping

Instructions:

1. **Make the Batter:** In a bowl, mix flour, water, garlic powder, and paprika to form a batter.
2. **Coat the Cauliflower:** Dip cauliflower florets in the batter to coat.
3. **Grill the Cauliflower:** Preheat grill to medium-high heat. Grill coated cauliflower for 10-12 minutes, turning occasionally. Toss in buffalo sauce before serving. Serve with blue cheese dressing if desired.

Enjoy your delicious grilled creations!

BBQ Duck Breasts

Ingredients:

- 2 duck breasts
- Salt and pepper to taste
- 1/4 cup BBQ sauce

Instructions:

1. **Prep the Duck:** Score the skin of the duck breasts in a crosshatch pattern and season with salt and pepper.
2. **Sear the Duck:** Preheat grill to medium-high heat. Place duck breasts skin-side down on the grill. Cook for about 6-8 minutes until the skin is crispy.
3. **Grill the Other Side:** Flip the breasts and cook for another 4-6 minutes for medium-rare. Brush with BBQ sauce during the last couple of minutes. Let rest before slicing.

Grilled Peach Salad

Ingredients:

- 2 ripe peaches, halved and pitted
- 4 cups mixed greens
- 1/2 cup feta cheese, crumbled
- 1/4 cup walnuts, toasted
- 2 tablespoons olive oil
- 1 tablespoon balsamic vinegar
- Salt and pepper to taste

Instructions:

1. **Grill the Peaches:** Preheat grill to medium heat. Grill peach halves for about 3-4 minutes until caramelized and grill marks appear.
2. **Assemble the Salad:** In a bowl, combine mixed greens, grilled peaches, feta, and walnuts. Drizzle with olive oil and balsamic vinegar, then season with salt and pepper.

Cilantro Lime Grilled Chicken

Ingredients:

- 4 chicken breasts
- 1/4 cup olive oil
- Juice of 2 limes
- 1/4 cup cilantro, chopped
- 2 cloves garlic, minced
- Salt and pepper to taste

Instructions:

1. **Marinate the Chicken:** In a bowl, whisk together olive oil, lime juice, cilantro, garlic, salt, and pepper. Add chicken and marinate for at least 30 minutes.
2. **Grill the Chicken:** Preheat grill to medium-high heat. Grill chicken for 6-7 minutes per side until cooked through.

Smoky BBQ Chili

Ingredients:

- 1 pound ground beef or turkey
- 1 onion, diced
- 2 cloves garlic, minced
- 1 can (15 oz) diced tomatoes
- 1 can (15 oz) kidney beans, drained
- 1 can (15 oz) black beans, drained
- 1 cup BBQ sauce
- 1 tablespoon smoked paprika
- Salt and pepper to taste

Instructions:

1. **Cook the Meat:** In a large pot, brown the ground meat with onion and garlic over medium heat until cooked through.
2. **Add Ingredients:** Stir in tomatoes, beans, BBQ sauce, smoked paprika, salt, and pepper. Simmer for about 20 minutes, stirring occasionally.

Grilled Romaine Salad

Ingredients:

- 2 heads romaine lettuce, halved lengthwise
- 2 tablespoons olive oil
- Salt and pepper to taste
- 1/2 cup Caesar dressing
- Grated Parmesan cheese for serving

Instructions:

1. **Prep the Lettuce:** Brush the cut sides of romaine with olive oil and season with salt and pepper.
2. **Grill the Lettuce:** Preheat grill to medium heat. Grill romaine for 2-3 minutes until charred.
3. **Serve:** Drizzle with Caesar dressing and top with Parmesan cheese.

BBQ Shrimp and Grits

Ingredients:

- 1 pound shrimp, peeled and deveined
- 1 cup grits
- 4 cups water or broth
- 1/4 cup BBQ sauce
- 1/2 cup cheddar cheese, shredded
- 2 tablespoons butter
- Salt and pepper to taste

Instructions:

1. **Cook the Grits:** In a pot, bring water or broth to a boil. Stir in grits and cook according to package instructions. Add cheese and butter, stirring until creamy. Season with salt and pepper.
2. **Cook the Shrimp:** In a skillet, add shrimp and BBQ sauce. Cook over medium heat for about 5 minutes until shrimp are cooked through.
3. **Serve:** Spoon grits into bowls and top with BBQ shrimp.

Sriracha Honey Grilled Chicken

Ingredients:

- 4 chicken thighs or breasts
- 2 tablespoons Sriracha
- 2 tablespoons honey
- 2 tablespoons soy sauce
- 1 tablespoon lime juice

Instructions:

1. **Make the Marinade:** In a bowl, whisk together Sriracha, honey, soy sauce, and lime juice. Add chicken and marinate for at least 30 minutes.
2. **Grill the Chicken:** Preheat grill to medium-high heat. Grill chicken for 6-7 minutes per side until cooked through, basting with leftover marinade.

Mediterranean Grilled Vegetable Platter

Ingredients:

- 1 zucchini, sliced
- 1 yellow squash, sliced
- 1 bell pepper, cut into strips
- 1 red onion, cut into wedges
- 1/4 cup olive oil
- 2 tablespoons balsamic vinegar
- Salt and pepper to taste
- Fresh herbs (oregano, thyme) for garnish

Instructions:

1. **Prep the Vegetables:** In a bowl, toss the vegetables with olive oil, balsamic vinegar, salt, and pepper.
2. **Grill the Vegetables:** Preheat grill to medium heat. Grill vegetables for about 10-15 minutes until tender and slightly charred.
3. **Serve:** Arrange on a platter and garnish with fresh herbs.

Enjoy your delicious BBQ meals!

BBQ Pulled Jackfruit Sandwiches

Ingredients:

- 2 cans young green jackfruit in water (not syrup), drained and rinsed
- 1 tablespoon olive oil
- 1 onion, diced
- 2 cloves garlic, minced
- 1 cup BBQ sauce
- Salt and pepper to taste
- Hamburger buns
- Optional toppings: coleslaw, pickles

Instructions:

1. **Prep the Jackfruit:** In a pot, heat olive oil over medium heat. Sauté onion and garlic until soft. Add jackfruit, breaking it apart with a fork.
2. **Cook:** Stir in BBQ sauce, salt, and pepper. Simmer for about 20 minutes until heated through and tender.
3. **Assemble Sandwiches:** Serve on buns with optional toppings.

Lemon Pepper Grilled Fish

Ingredients:

- 4 fish fillets (such as tilapia or salmon)
- 2 tablespoons olive oil
- Juice of 1 lemon
- 1 teaspoon lemon pepper seasoning
- Salt to taste

Instructions:

1. **Marinate the Fish:** In a bowl, whisk together olive oil, lemon juice, lemon pepper seasoning, and salt. Coat fish fillets and marinate for 15-30 minutes.
2. **Grill the Fish:** Preheat grill to medium heat. Grill fish for about 4-5 minutes per side until cooked through and flaky.

Chipotle BBQ Corn Salad

Ingredients:

- 4 ears of corn, husked and grilled
- 1 can (15 oz) black beans, rinsed and drained
- 1 red bell pepper, diced
- 1/4 cup red onion, diced
- 1/4 cup cilantro, chopped
- 1/4 cup chipotle BBQ sauce
- Juice of 1 lime
- Salt to taste

Instructions:

1. **Grill the Corn:** Preheat grill to medium heat. Grill corn for about 10-15 minutes until charred. Let cool, then cut kernels off the cob.
2. **Mix the Salad:** In a bowl, combine corn, black beans, bell pepper, red onion, cilantro, chipotle BBQ sauce, lime juice, and salt. Toss to combine.

Grilled Sweet Potatoes

Ingredients:

- 2 large sweet potatoes, sliced into rounds
- 2 tablespoons olive oil
- Salt and pepper to taste
- Optional: paprika or cayenne for spice

Instructions:

1. **Prep the Sweet Potatoes:** Toss sweet potato slices with olive oil, salt, pepper, and optional spices.
2. **Grill the Sweet Potatoes:** Preheat grill to medium heat. Grill sweet potatoes for about 6-8 minutes per side until tender and charred.

BBQ Chicken Nachos

Ingredients:

- 2 cups cooked chicken, shredded
- 1 cup BBQ sauce
- Tortilla chips
- 1 cup shredded cheese (cheddar or Monterey Jack)
- 1/4 cup jalapeños (optional)
- Optional toppings: sour cream, green onions, cilantro

Instructions:

1. **Prepare the Chicken:** Mix shredded chicken with BBQ sauce.
2. **Assemble Nachos:** On a baking sheet, layer tortilla chips, BBQ chicken, cheese, and jalapeños.
3. **Bake or Grill:** Preheat grill to medium heat or oven to 350°F (175°C). Cook for about 10-15 minutes until cheese is melted. Serve with toppings.

Smoked Mac and Cheese

Ingredients:

- 1 pound elbow macaroni
- 4 tablespoons butter
- 1/4 cup flour
- 4 cups milk
- 3 cups shredded cheese (cheddar, mozzarella, or a mix)
- 1 teaspoon smoked paprika
- Salt and pepper to taste
- Optional: breadcrumbs for topping

Instructions:

1. **Cook the Macaroni:** Cook macaroni according to package instructions and set aside.
2. **Make the Cheese Sauce:** In a pot, melt butter, stir in flour, and cook for 1 minute. Gradually add milk, stirring until thickened. Mix in cheese, paprika, salt, and pepper until smooth.
3. **Combine and Smoke:** Mix cooked macaroni with cheese sauce. Pour into a smoking-safe dish, top with breadcrumbs if desired, and smoke at 225°F (107°C) for about 30-45 minutes.

Enjoy your delicious BBQ meals!

www.ingramcontent.com/pod-product-compliance
Lightning Source LLC
LaVergne TN
LVHW081323060526
838201LV00055B/2424